Ukulele Songs For Beginners

Folk & Country Tunes

Frederick Johnson

Copyright © 2019 Frederick Johnson

Ukulele Chords Reference Guide

CONTENTS

UKULELE SONGS FOR BEGINNERS
Folk & Country Tunes

Introduction

Welcome to the ukulele and let me start by saying well done and a massive congratulations for choosing what Jake Shimabukuro (the world's most successful ukulele player) called the instrument of peace. Indeed how right he was and soon, you'll see just why the ukulele has become the most popular instrument to learn. These days, you find a lot of tutorials and lessons on the internet but what you won't find there is an in depth guide from day one to explain to you all the basics of the ukulele and give you step by step tuition. That is what this book is for: to provide you with an insightful and easy peasy method of playing the ukulele from the moment you open the box and hold the instrument in your hands for the very first time.

In this chapter, you will be given an introduction to your instrument. This involves a breakdown of the individual parts that make up the ukulele, some basic maintenance tips and preparing you to start strumming away.

What is a ukulele?

We will start by giving an overview of what a ukulele actually is. Many falsely believe that the ukulele is related to the guitar and therefore is part of the guitar family. Others believe that the ukulele is a stand alone instrument whereby it is unique as a construction and no other instruments like it exist. This is also a false misconception.

The truth is that the ukulele is a family of instruments. The uke comes in four sizes: soprano, concert, tenor and baritone. With the increase in demand for stringed instrument production and with advances in recent luthier technology, new hybrids have also emerged such as the guitarlele which is a six string ukulele. This instrument was designed to help guitarists make an easy transition to the ukulele without actually having to learn the ukulele since the instrument has the same intonation as a guitar but tuned a fifth higher. The bass ukulele is another such hybrid. Nevertheless, the chances are that if you're starting the ukulele, you own a soprano since this is the most common kind. Psst… we think it's the best kind too.

So let us now take a look at the different parts of the ukulele and what each component is for.

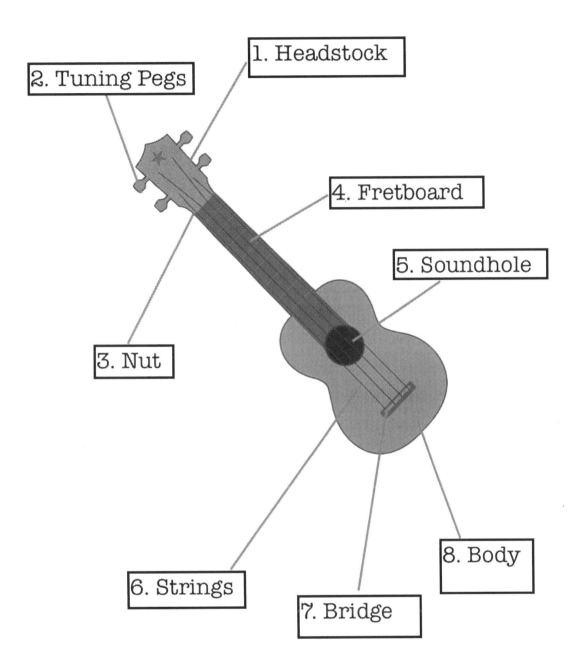

1. Headstock

2. Tuning Pegs

4. Fretboard

5. Soundhole

3. Nut

8. Body

6. Strings

7. Bridge

─────────────────────────────────────-Index────────────────────────────

1. Headstock

The function of the headstock is to contain the tuning pegs and to balance the ukulele's weight appropriately for an overall accurate intonation.

The headstock is a fragile part of the instrument which you should avoid knocking or hitting at all costs. This point cannot be emphasised enough. Since ukuleles are delicate in that they are smaller than most stringed instruments and have a tighter neck and string tension, even a single heavy knock can cause severe or even permanent damage to the instrument. Such damage can vary from your ukulele no longer staying in tune to a dented neck or even fret and nut problems. Any of these will cost you a lot of money, especially since ukulele repair is a niche field which not all guitar luthiers may be able to pull off successfully. It's best to take precautionary measures and look after your instrument. Purchase a gig bag or case for all transportation.

2. Tuning Pegs

There are four tuning pegs on the ukulele, one for each string. Ukulele tuning pegs are extremely sensitive and so when you are tuning your instrument, especially if you got your instrument new with no setup and loose strings, be extremely cautious as ukulele strings snap HARD if you tune incorrectly and are careless. Tune each peg slowly, turning them progressively - never in quick motions. Since guitars have longer necks than ukuleles, you can afford to tune in swift motions. Ukuleles are smaller and have a shorter distance between the strings and the headstock. Therefore, they tighten quickly. Bear this in mind when first tuning your new instrument.

3. Nut

The nut is often overlooked and some players do not take into consideration just how pivotal this little bit of material really is. The nut is the linking point between the strings, bridge and headstock. It contains four individual slits where the strings sit on. Damage to the nut is as bad as damage to the headstock, if not worse. What you must appreciate as a ukulele player is that while the nut seems futile, those individually spaced slits have been measured apart in a precise way down to the last millimetre. It is actually one of the most strenuous and laborious aspects of the craftsmanship that goes into fabrication of the instrument. When replacing strings, take your time and if you are ever unsure, have them replaced by your local music shop. Better to be safe than sorry.

4. Fretboard

The fretboard is the actual part of the instrument that your notation is played on. If you are right-handed, your left hand navigates this part of the ukulele. Ensure the frets (individually lined notes) are not sharp and are smooth. If there are any issues, make sure to address them professionally before playing as injuries are frequent in poorly constructed and set up ukuleles. Most guitar stores will be able to sort out minor issues. The fretboard sits on the neck which your hand grasps as you play.

5. Soundhole

The sound hole is pretty self explanatory. It's where sound emits out of the instrument when played. On acoustic guitars, it's where many people accidentally drop their picks into (*'plectrum'* for our lovely British and Australian readers). Nonetheless, be sure that nothing is inside the sound hole as this can impair performance and the overall sound of your ukulele.

6. Strings

Let's now talk about the strings of the ukulele. Similar to   classical guitars, ukuleles use nylon or gut strings. We will talk specifically about the tuning of the ukulele in the next section of the book. Be aware that your strings should never feel too tight agains the fretboard of the ukulele. There should be an ease where you are able to press down on each fret and bend the strings a little bit. A maintenance tip is to purchase a guitar cleaning kit. These are inexpensive and usually contain conditioner. Keeping your strings clean is essential for hygiene and a crisp sounding instrument. Alternatively, use a duster and dab a small amount of water on a tea towel to regularly clean your fretboard and strings.

7. Bridge

The bridge is what holds the strings in place on the opposite end of the ukulele to the headstock. Don't mess around with this part of the ukulele as much like the other components which involve maintaining correct string tension, it is extremely delicate. You might note that the strings are tied in a knot on the bridge and unlike guitars, there are no pinned 'slots' in the bridge where you can insert strings into easily. This means that changing strings is not something you should try at home unless you are proficient in ukulele string replacement. Ask a guitar or music shop to do this for you when you do eventually buy new strings.

8. Body

Finally, the most prominent feature of your ukulele: its body. Look after it and ensure to dust it from time to time. Dust culminates a lot on the body's outer rim, the headstock and on top of the strings. Just like with any part of the instrument, ensure no physical damage occurs on it and love your instrument like you love any other personal expensive property.

Tuning Up

Now that we have covered the basics of the instrument, it's time to start playing. The key to all good performance is a well tuned ukulele. Ukulele tuning is similar to other four stringed instruments but is very unique as the second string (the C string) is lower in pitch than the other strings. This is rare in stringed fretted instruments.

Ukulele tuning looks like this:

G   **C**   **E**   **A**

In tablature form (which we will look at very shortly), it looks like this:

```
A|-- - --|
E|-      - --|
C|-          |
G|-          |
```

Tablature

On the previous page, you were shown what we call tablature. Tablature is the full word for what are often known as 'tabs'. This is far more commonly used these days. Tablature is sheet music for ukulele and other stringed instruments. It shows us what notes we have to play through numbers on different strings. In ukulele tabs, the G note (the lowest string which is also closest to you) is the bottom string, the C note the next one along and so on.

The first thing that I would like you to do is to play each note openly: G to A.

In tablature, playing each note openly would look like this:

The reason for the 0 is that we aren't actually playing on a fret. The numbers demonstrate which fret we have to put our fingers on. An open string is always marked as a 0 in tablature.

It is time now for our first lesson. In this lesson, we will play a very simple pattern and you will see how it looks when we tab it out.

Lesson:

For this lesson, you will be using the G string only.

Step 1: Play the open G string.

Step 2: Place your index finger (or middle finger) on the   second fret of the G string and play it. The second fret is the second note away from the nut which is marked by the frets (the lines on the fretboard).

Step 3: Let go and play the G string open again.

We started with a 0 on the G string which marked the fact you played the string open. This was followed by the 2 which means you played the second fret and then we have a 0 again where a string is played openly. Now we are going to include other strings.

This might look intimidating at first but it really is something you are capable of performing with the knowledge you have acquired so far. Don't worry, I will guide you through.

Step 1: Start the tune by playing the G string open.

Step 2: Just like in the previous exercise, place your finger on the second fret of the G string.

Step 3: Now you want to place your ring finger on the fifth fret of the C string and pluck it.

Step 4: Next, place your index finger on the second fret of the C string.

Step 5: Finish the melody by playing the C string open.

The key is to practice this shift over and over until you get the hang of switching between strings. Try switching between other strings as well. We will look at one more exercise in basic tablature before learning chords which use tablature.

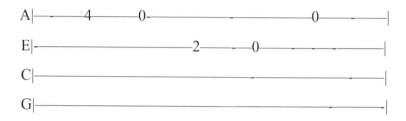

The focus on the previous exercises was on the lower strings. Now we move to the higher strings. This exercise is admittedly more challenging but you can do it. Take it slowly at first and do not rush. Speed comes with time and practice. What is more important is that you play the melody accurately and read the tabs correctly.

Step 1: We start by playing the fourth fret of the A string. Use your ring finger.

Step 2: Then play the A string open.

Step 3: Place your index finger on the second fret of the E string and then play it open.

Step 4: Finish the melody by playing the open A string.

Practice the melody and in your own time, speed up as much as you deem appropriate based on what sounds right to you. It might seem hard at first to group these notes together into a sequence but you'll get there as you improve with repetition.

Separate notes vs grouped notes

Another important element of reading tablature is when you see notes grouped together versus separate. Let's take a look at what this distinction entails.

Look at the two pieces of tablature on the following page. Can you spot the difference?

Diagram (a)

Diagram (b)

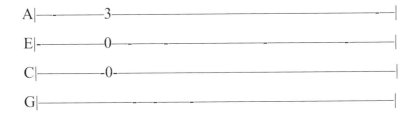

Both diagrams involve the same group of notes: the open C and E strings with the third fret of the A string. However, there is indeed a vital difference between these two diagrams. This is the spacing. When notes are separated as demonstrated in *diagram (a)*, the notes are meant to be played individually and not strummed as a chord. In other words, each note should be picked separately. In this case, you would start by playing the C string, then the E string and finishing on the A string respectively.

In the case of *diagram (b)*, the notes are in line with each other which we call a chord. The notes are meant to be strummed in unison. So instead of playing each note separately, you would have your index or middle finger on the third fret of the A string before playing any note. Then, you would strum the C, E and A strings together. We will come onto chords very shortly but keep in mind the difference between a sequence of notes and grouped notes. One little exercise you can try out is play *diagram (a)* and *(b)* one after the other. Familiarising yourself with the feel of different methods of ukulele playing in the initial stages is the difference between accelerating quickly and learning slower than you could otherwise learn.

One more example to illustrate this point would be as follows:

Diagram (c)

Diagram (d)

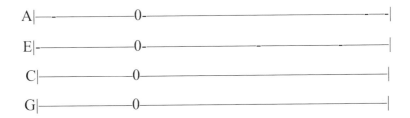

As we observed in the first two diagrams, diagram (c) is the individual notation and diagram (d) represents the grouped notes. This example is a mile simpler however as it is all open notes. Diagram (c) asks of us only to play through each note one by one whereas diagram (d) demands us to strum every string together and open. Hopefully this is simple enough.

Now it's time to look at chords.

Chords

Chords are groups of notes (typically between *2* and *5* notes) strummed in unison. In this chapter, you will be introduced to basic chord shapes and then you will learn how to play them together to form what are called **chord progressions**.

Chords are a step up from individual tabs since multiple notes are being played in one single strum plus there is the added expense of having to pick correctly and then change shape.

Do not fret! (n*o pun intended*) This chapter will help you with all of the potential hurdles and before you know it, you'll be jamming away through songs with ease. Be patient, practice each exercise and take your time. Learning chords on ukulele can be a frustrating process but keep with it. It is worth the hard work that you put in.

We'll be looking at the following chords to start off with :

C major, G major, A minor and F major.

We will begin with the chord that all beginners ought to know like the back of their hand. The *C major* chord.

This is what the chord looks like when written out. C major on the ukulele is the simplest chord to play since it only involves one finger being used.

Step 1: To start the chord, place your index finger (pointer) on the third fret of the A string.

Step 2: Strum the C, E and A strings. i.e. the top three strings of the ukulele.

If you got it right, you should hear the beautiful sound of a C chord.

Do not move on to the next chord until you have a good grasp of the C chord. An exercise which you must learn to do is to play a new chord and then remove all your fingers from the instrument. After a few seconds, try to re-find the fingering and play the chord again from memory. This method, employed by top musicians (particularly guitarists) helps your muscle memory increase drastically. It is arduous at first but the more you try it, the better you'll get the hang of it.

Our second chord is the **G major** chord.

```
A|--  --         2                              |
E|-              3-- -              -        --  |
C|           - --2-       -  - -                 |
G|            -0                                 |
```

So right off the bat, I'm going to be completely honest with you: on every stringed instrument whether it be the mandolin, guitar or ukulele, the G chord has a way of somehow being the most frustrating chord to learn. Unfortunately, we have to roll with it and just face it head on. Again, once you learn the fingering for the chord, repeat the shape as hard as it may be. Muscle memory never fails a ukulele player!

Step 1: Place your index finger on the second fret of the C string.

Step 2: Place your ring finger (yes I know it feels weird) on the third fret of the E string.

Step 3: Finish with the middle finger tucked underneath it on the A string.

If you ever saw the 90s sitcom **Friends**, this is the chord shape that Phoebe called the 'bear claw' because your fingers resemble those of a creature with scrunched paws. Or maybe even Yoda from Star Wars…

Exercise

Before moving on to the third chord, it is time for an exercise. We have covered two essential chords and it would benefit you to focus on these before moving on. To really make these chords stick in your memory, you need to put them into practical use. So we are going to practice an exercise whereby you will play the C chord and the G chord in sequence as   follows.

C   *G*   *C*   *G*

Take your time with it ! Practice it until it flows naturally and then move on to the next chord shape. It's important to practice every chord as you go along as opposed to cramming them in later. The more you become used to associating a chord name with its shape, the easier you'll find practicing songs later on when you have no visual prompter or tab to help you.

C

G

C

G

```
A|--------------------2-----------------------------------------|
E|--------------------3-----------------------------------------|
C|--------------------2-----------------------------------------|
G|------------------0------------------------------------------|
```

Our third chord shape is A minor. This is similar to the C chord in that it involves a singe finger on the fretting hand.

Step 1: To play this chord, begin by placing your index finger or middle finger (if you prefer) in the second fret of the G string.

Step 2: That's pretty much it. Now you strum the four strings.

If you are new to music, minor chords are supposed to sound sad and they act really well with major chords (the 'happy' sounding chords). In modern pop music, you typically find one minor chord in a progression of four chords but we will come onto chord progressions in due course.

Exercise

It is time for an exercise again. At this point, having learned three chords: one of which was a pretty challenging one, we need to practice bringing them together and incorporating the A minor with the two major chords.

For this exercise, we are going to play a chord progression. It is simpler than it looks so give it as much of a chance as you can. Play it slowly and take as much time as you need to switch chord shapes.

The progression is:

C   G   *Am*   C

In this sequence, we are starting out on a C major chord, moving to G, then the A minor (which is arguably the most uphill part of this exercise) and then back to C. It's a challenge   because shifting from a three finger chord to a one finger chord can be quite an experience when starting out. This exercise is not random nor pointless though because practicing it and   getting a grasp of it will help you with three key aspects of ukulele playing.

1. Switching between chords.
2. Muscle memory and increased finger agility.
3. Returning back to the key note (C) after having played other chords.

Point three is particularly indispensable because in any genre of music, it is one thing to be able to switch chords but what makes a musician particularly skilled is the ability to return to the starting chord/note having gone through the progression. In this case, C major is your anchor. Focus on points 1 and 2 but also put extra practice into going from the G major and A minor back to the C major.

C

```
A|--  ------3--------------------------------------------------|
E|-----------------0-----  -----------  ---------  ------|
C|-----------------0-----------------------------------------|
G|----------------------------------------  ----------  --|
```

G

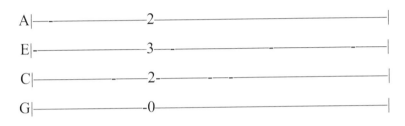

```
A|--  ------2--------------------------------------------------|
E|----------------3----  -----------  ----------  ------|
C|----------------2---  --------------------------------------|
G|-----------------0-----------------------------------------|
```

Am

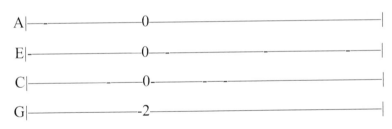

```
A|--  ------0--------------------------------------------------|
E|-------------0-----  -----------  ----------  ------|
C|-------------0--  ----------------------------------------|
G|-------------2---------------------------------------------|
```

C

```
A|--  ------3--------------------------------------------------|
E|-----------0-----  -----------  ----------  ------|
C|----------0--------------------------------------------|
G|---------------------------------------  ----------  --|
```

The next chord we will look at is the F major chord.

This chord can appear to be quite tricky but if you nail this one down, you'll really be making progress in your ukulele   journey. The F major chord uses two fingers in what is actually quite a stretch if you're brand new. Don't panic though because you will get there. As repetitive as I have been about it: practice will make you the best uke player you can be.

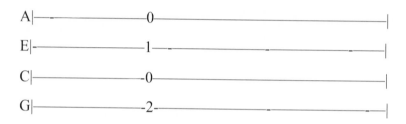

The F chord is different to the previous chords we have looked at because the leading finger which for a lot of chords is typically the index finger, is actually the middle finger.

Step 1: Start by placing your middle finger on the second fret of the G string.

Step 2: Keeping the G string firmly pressed down, place your index finger on the first fret of the E string. Remember, we are skipping a string so be sure you aren't placing your index finger on the first fret of the C string otherwise you will get an A   major chord which is fine but NOT what we are going for here.

If you're starting out, do not be disheartened if you find this fingering particularly difficult. You aren't expected to perfect the F major chord when you're just a few days into playing. However, in your own time and without rushing, do try to memorise the shape of the F chord. Another good exercise is performing the shape away from the instrument and just in your day to day life. The muscles in your hand will strengthen and become used to the stretch.

The final chord which we will look at is the D major chord. I wish I had better news for you but this chord is another tough one. Still, you need to be introduced to these chords   because while they can be hard, they are essential and the D major chord is one of the most recurring chords in music.

```
A|----------------5-------------------------------|
E|---------------2------------------          -----|
C|---------------2---------------------------------|
G|---------------------------------------     ----|
```

The D major is a three finger chord.

Step 1: Place your index finger on the second fret of the C string.

Step 2: Place your middle finger just underneath it on the second fret of the E string.

Step 3: Now for the stretch. Place your pinky finger (*yes that's right: pinky finger*) on the fifth fret of the A string. Strum the chord.

You might be aware that the chord looks a bit peculiar. It's probably because you are leaving a two fret gap. Don't worry, it's meant to feel and look like that. Strum the entire chord making sure your index and middle finger are not muting each other. If your fingers are muting these strings a bit, it's because your shape needs to be more accurate.

Accurate fingerings are what make the ukulele sound crisp and professional. If you do find yourself in a situation of buzzing or muting, bend the fingers a little bit and make sure you are pressing hard enough on the string. There will be a little bit of pain if you are new to stringed fretted instruments but your finger tips will callus with time and practice and no longer cause any issues.

We have now covered the basic chords needed when starting out on the ukulele. There are many other chords which you need to learn and they are included on the opening page so   please do refer to the diagram and learn some of the other chords at your own volition. I would recommend looking at the A major chord and B minor chord to begin with.

A major

B minor

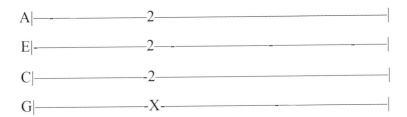

In the B minor chord, you might be wondering what the X is. In tablature, when you see an X, it signifies that you do not play that string at all.

With what's been covered so far, you should have all the knowledge and skill required to teach yourself some of the   other chord shapes so don't be shy or intimidated, you can do it and I believe you will be an awesome ukulele player who is going to be able to play any chord on demand in no time!

Chord Progressions

Chord progressions put the chords you've learned into practice and turn sound into music. We have already looked at a few with the C, G and A minor chords.

Here are a few for you to try out:

1. C   F   C   G   C

2. C   G   Am   F

3. D   G   G   D

4. Am   F   C   G   C

5. F   G   F   G   C

6. C   Am   G   Am   C

7. C   D   C   G   C

8. C   C   F   Am   C

Strumming

When first starting out on the ukulele or any stringed instrument for that matter, it is tempting to just strum downwards. However, the earlier you learn how to strum properly, the quicker you'll pick it up. Ukulele players determine how to strum their instrument based on strumming patterns. That is, when the strum downwards and upwards in different amounts. For example, a typical strum is:

down   down   up

(D   D   U)

This means that the player, with their right hand, will strum down twice and back up once. Strumming down means starting at the bottom string (G) and moving down while hitting all four strings and letting them ring out at once. Strumming upwards involves starting with the high string (A) and doing the same thing as down-strumming but in reverse.

Songs rarely start with an up-strum and typically begin with a down-strum. You can practice strumming slowly and build it up to a normal speed. This is an effective way to practice. Don't feel discouraged if you don't get it at first.

It does take time to perfect it and soon, you'll be able to strum to all sorts of strumming patterns. Here are three common strumming patterns that you will come across.

(I recommend that you start practicing these patterns on one chord first before playing multiple chords. Once you feel you've got the hang of it, try two chords and then three or four. After, you may apply strumming patterns to the previous exercises).

D. D. U. D. U. D

(x4)

D. U. D. U. D. U. D. U

(x4)

D. U. D. D. U

(x4)

Folk & Country Tunes

Cherish The Ladies
(Traditional Celtic Jig)

Champion's Jig

```
A|———0———————————————————————————————————————————|
E|————————————————2———2———2———————————————————————|
C|—————————————————————————————————————————————————|
G|—————————————————————————————————————————————————|
```

The Castle Gardens

Anderson's Jig

```
A|————————————-10——————-    ———————————————————————————|
E|———————— -  —  —  —  —  ———————7——————————  —————————|
C|——————————————————————  —  ——————————————  —————————|
G|————————7————  ————————————————————————————————————|
```

Thomas Fell In The Pond

(Cornish Jig)

```
A|----------------------------------------------------------|
E|------------3---------------------------------------------|
C|--------0----------------------------------------------- -|
G|------0---------------------------------------------------|


A|-----------3--------5------------3------------------------|
E|----------------------------------------------------------|
C|----------------------------------------------------------|
G|----------------------------------------------------------|


A|----------------------------------------------------------|
E|---------5----------------3-------------------------------|
C|----------------------------------------------------------|
G|----------------------------------------------------------|


A|------------------3----------5----------------------------|
E|------5--------------------5------------------------------|
C|----------------------------------------------------------|
G|----------------------------------------------------------|
```

Midwestern Jig

(Unknown Origin: Traditional)

```
A|--------------------------------------------------------------|
E|-------------------------3--------5---------------------------|
C|-----2---------4----------------------------------------------|
G|--------------------------------------------------------------|


A|-----3--------------------------------------------------------|
E|--------------------------5-----------------------------------|
C|--------------------------------------------------------------|
G|--------------------------------------------------------------|


A|--------------------------------------------------------------|
E|--------------------------------------------------------------|
C|-----0---------------2-------------0--------------------------|
G|--------------------------------------------------------------|


A|--------------------------------------------------------------|
E|--------------------------------------------------------------|
C|-----2---------4-------------0--------------------------------|
G|--------------------------------------------------------------|
```

She Said I Wonder When

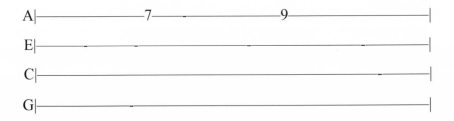

```
A|————————————————-——————————————————————————|
E|————-7————-————9————-————————10——————-———-————|
C|————————————————————————————-——————————-————|
G|———————————————-——————————-——————————————————|
```

```
A|————————————————-——————————————————————————|
E|————9————————————7————————5————————5———————————|
C|—————————————————————————————————————-—-————|
G|——————————————-————————————————————————————|
```

Dakota Tribute

Home Sweet Home

(Scottish Jig)

```
A|————————————————————————————————————2————————————————————|
E|—————————————————————————3————————————————————————————————|
C|————————2——————————————————————————————————————————————————|
G|————————————————————————————————————————————————————————————|


A|————————————————————————————————————0————————————————————|
E|—————————————————————————3——————————————————————————————|
C|————————4——————————————————————————————————————————————————|
G|————————————————————————————————————————————————————————————|


A|————————————————————————————————————0————————————————————|
E|—————————————————————————2——————————————————————————————|
C|————————3——————————————————————————————————————————————————|
G|————————————————————————————————————————————————————————————|


A|————————————————————————————————————2————————————————————|
E|—————————————————————————3——————————————————————————————|
C|————————4——————————————————————————————————————————————————|
G|————————————————————————————————————————————————————————————|
```

I Saw The Spirit In The Wind

St. Anne's Glory

Arizona Freedom

Made in the USA
Middletown, DE
30 November 2023

44094861R00068